Auras

The complete guide to auras, seeing auras, feeling auras, sensing auras, and understanding auras and astral colors!

Table Of Contents

Introduction 1
Free Bonus 2
Chapter 1: What is an Aura? 3
Chapter 2: How to See the Aura 9
Chapter 3: The Colors of the Aura 12
Chapter 4: How to Feel the Aura 24
Chapter 5: The Different Layers of The Aura 27
Chapter 6: Strategies for Seeing Auras 31
Chapter 7: Auras of Different Things and Animals 36
Chapter 8: How to Change and Improve Your Aura 38
Chapter 9: How to See Your Own Aura 41
Conclusion 43

Introduction

I want to thank you and congratulate you for taking the time to read this book on auras! This is the recently updated 2nd edition. I can now proudly present this book as the complete guide to getting started with Auras!

This book contains helpful information about auras, what they are, and how you can begin seeing them!

You will soon discover the history of auras, and how they have been observed in many cultures, as well as in a scientific sense.

You will learn about the different meanings of auras, and how the colors can change depending on mood, health, the situation, time of day, and more!

Not only will you learn how to begin seeing auras on objects, people, and yourself, you will also discover how to feel and sense them.

This book will explain to you tips and techniques that will allow you to successfully understand and begin seeing auras today! This includes auras of objects, plants, animals, other people, and even yourself!

Whether you're a skeptic of auras, or are a firm believer, this book will have something to offer you in the way of insight, and ability.

Thanks again for picking up this book, I hope you enjoy it!

Free Bonus

As a thank you for taking the time to download my book, I'd like to offer you a **FREE** bonus!

I have compiled a list of my '7 Keys For Successful Meditation', and have made it free for you to download.

You can CLICK HERE to claim your free copy, or click on the link below:

http://bit.ly/1F91lfl

Meditation helps you to clear and focus your mind, and allows you to gain better control over your thoughts and focus. Regular meditation can make it a lot easier to successfully engage in things like Reiki healing, aura viewing, and opening your third eye, as these all involve deep and powerful use of your mind and focus.

So download my free report today – CLICK HERE – and begin experiencing the amazing benefits of meditation today!

Chapter 1:
What is an Aura?

Perhaps you have heard of the concept of the aura at least once in your life. However, you may either have several misconceptions about this concept, or may may not believe it entirely. But the aura is as real as it gets, and this book will show you not only proof of its existence, but will also help you see it for yourself.

First off, an aura is something that surrounds all living things -- even that tree in your backyard, or your pet kitten. However, only humans have enough sophistication to be able to actually utilize it to its full extent, and sense it in others. It is basically an egg-shaped layer of colors that surrounds a person. This layer is also called a psychic energy field -- it is basically a "fingerprint" that shows not only your specific personality, but also what you feel at the exact moment someone reads your aura.

The art and science of aura reading involves not only the observation, but also the accurate interpretation of auras. It is something that takes considerable practice, but its fruits are extremely rewarding.

The aura, also, is not just one solid block of colors -- it is a perpetually changing and swirling field with multiple layers; how many layers there are will depend on the source, though many settle on three to seven. The area that these layers occupy also changes from time to time (or from mood to mood), and can be as large as three feet from the person to as narrow as only a few inches outward. The intensity and brightness may also differ, marking important changes.

This book will tell you more about the intricacies of these layers and the colors associated with auras, as well as how they can be observed and interpreted.

Auras in Different Beliefs

Unbeknownst to many people, the concept of the aura can actually be seen in several different belief systems across the world. Oftentimes, the aura is associated with a person who has special qualities that are representative of their belief's values.

Zoroastrianism

In this religion, especially among its followers in and around Iran, the concept of the aura is commonly called "farr" which means "glory". Zoroastrian kings are usually associated with this symbol, and their depictions usually show the aura as a flame-like design enveloping the person.

Buddhism

In the Buddhist flag itself (which contains the colors blue, yellow, red, white, and orange), the concept of the aura is solidly embodied. According to the adherents of the belief, the flag represents the different colors that were seen around the enlightened Buddha.

Jainism

In Jainism, the concept of the aura is embodied in their "Lesya", which is the Jain theory on karma and the soul. This refers to the colors manifested by the soul in direct association with karmic matter, mental, and emotional dispositions.

Hinduism

In Hinduism, the aura is associated with a person's mental and emotional impressions. The practice of spiritual growth gradually turns this aura into a halo. In their traditions (as well as that of the Buddhists), the color of the aura is somehow related to the chakras, as well as to the Kundalini energy. Kundalini energy in itself refers to the kind of spiritual energy that is awakened in the body's subtle system.

Kabbalah

In the tradition of Kabbalah, the aura is considered as an emanation or luster that comes from the astral body, associated with different mental faculties in an intricate system.

Christianism and Islamism

In the Christian and Islam religions, a symbolism of light mimics the effects of an aura. This is usually shown surrounding the head of a holy person as a halo, or covering the entire body of a heavenly being.

Theosophy, Anthrosophy, Archeosophy

In these esoteric traditions, each color that is associated with the aura means or indicates a precise state of a person's emotions. In fact, theosophist Charles Leadbeater has published an entire work that details the different chromatic manifestations of the aura, together with their individual meanings.

Other Traditions

British occultist W.E. Butler believed in the two different types of auras: the spiritual and the etheric. Aside from resembling the different mental and emotional states, the aura is also thought to be a measure of the physical body's state of health.

On the other hand, mystic author Robert Bruce classified the aura into three: the etheric, the spiritual, and the main auras. According to him, the aura is not really light per se but a visual translation of other unknown sensory readings that are added to our observations of a living being. These auras cannot be seen when there is complete darkness, and cannot be seen as well unless the source of it is visible.

British author and healer Paul Lambillion further elaborated on the aura as three layers in an "aural field" that can be observed even when the person is not personally present (i.e., when the source of the aura is seen on TV).

Glenn Morris, a noted martial artist, also included the concept of the aura in his teachings. According to him, advanced martial artists can gain a considerable advantage if they are able to perceive the aura of their opponents. He also mentioned that the aura consists of multiple layers -- with the most visible being a "light and denser than air" manifestation, usually at half an inch long. He also mentioned a yard-long and egg-shaped layer that was supposed to represent the person's hormonal levels, as well as other outer layers consisting of the mental state and others.

In the art of holistic healing, the aura plays a great role in investigating the patient's energy field. It is the basis of certain techniques, including but not limited to practices such as energy medicine, energy psychology, energy spirituality, and bioenergetics.

Scientific Tests

Many people refute the concept of the aura as fallacious and unscientific, often citing that the aura cannot be observed or captured in a scientific manner. However, back in 2013, a group of Japanese scientists hailing from the University of Tokyo have managed to scientifically capture the visible region of a person's aura. Led by Mio Watanabe, the researchers conducted a series of experiments detailing a person's "special glow," demonstrating its dynamic properties as it seems to grow dimmer as evening approaches. The experiment also revealed that the aura is most visible around a person's mouth, cheeks, neck, and face. They have investigated this as a diagnostic tool, believing that the presence of a certain type of aura around a certain body part may mean the presence of a disease or health issue.

One of the most common techniques for capturing a person's aura is called Kirlian photography, named after Semyon Kirlian, a Russian electrical engineer. The technique is also known as "Electrography", "electrophotography", or "gas discharge visualization (GDV)".

When the technique was first publicized, the couple noticed that the human body was capable of producing varied aural images. These images determined the total activity of the body, allowing a person who uses the technique to determine the efficiency of certain types of medications. It was also used to determine the conditions of certain organs and body systems. The images produced by the technique are both objectively and qualitatively evaluated, reducing the risk of any misinterpretations. The entire process is dependent on the light emissions coming from high-voltage electromagnetic fields.

Criticisms

The main criticism towards the concept of auras lies in the fact that many scientific groups are unable to replicate certain experiments purporting to have verified the aura's existence. There are several experiments using people who are supposedly "aura readers," but most of the time they are only able to only make marginally correct readings. While these failures can be due to mistakes in the experimental design, it is also possible that the participant "aura reader" may not be skilled in this trade at all. Some of these tests have even been televised.

In a review featured in the Skeptical Inquirer, Bridgette Perez had stated that the perception of auras may most likely be due to "perceptual distortions" and other factors including illusions, fantasy proneness, hallucinations, and even afterimages. While this may be true in some, it does not account for scientific equipment being able to detect the phenomenon.

There is at least one scientific phenomenon when the presence of an "aura" around things a person sees can be a sign of an illness. This is in the matter of synesthesia, when certain visual images appear to be seen even though they are non-existent. This usually comes in the form of automatically associating a certain color to a certain person, letter, or other object, even though there is no logical link in the association.

Chapter 2:
How to See the Aura

The fact of the matter is that an aura is a part of human existence in itself. Ask practitioners and they will immediately point out that they are able to see an aura because they are able to see the totality of the human person -- as each person possesses more than one body, aside from the corporeal one that we readily see. An aura is a tangible "other" part of everyone.

Here are a few steps that will help you see the aura, no matter what your faith or belief system may be:

1. **Believe.** This is usually the first and hardest obstacle to overcome. Normally, people operate by the tenet of "seeing is believing," whereby we do not lend any credibility to something that isn't obvious. Just remember how people of old ridiculed Columbus for his belief that the Earth is round!

   However, as it is with almost every part of psychic development, believing is actually seeing. This same tenet holds true in the development of ESP, psychic perceptions, etc. For this moment, we will use it in the field of aura reading. The layer of reality that has to do with energies (like the aura) is extremely subtle, and one needs to actually believe its existence first before being able to see it. In short, being open-minded is a prerequisite for success in this endeavor. This works in the basic mechanisms of human psychology: once people do not recognize something, they will not do anything to further their experience and understanding on the matter.

Of course, we are not telling you to blindly believe anything your spiritual guide tells you, or anything in this book whatsoever -- open-minded skepticism is always the best approach! Always give the benefit of the doubt until you actually discover the facts firsthand. It is true that in the psychic journey, not many people take the exact same route -- this may be one of the reasons we have so many branches and techniques even for the most basic of psychic processes!

2. **Do the work.** There is another thing that most people do not learn when they start their psychic journeys. They simply believe that everything will come in the blink of an eye, much like an epiphany. Truth is, this is very rarely the case (unless, of course, you have a real psychic predisposition – a rare gift).

   For a lot of those in training, existing beliefs, especially the religious kind, can be a huge progress-blocker. There are many who grew up thinking that this sort of practice is "magic" and therefore "evil," regardless if it was made to be done for the welfare of everyone involved. Daily meditation, energy work, and different types of psychic exercises are great catalysts on your way to aura reading.

3. **Take "Photographs".** While the first two steps mentioned were meant to prepare your "gear" for your aural readings, this step will propel you right into the midst of the process. Remember that psychic visions (aural readings included) are not seen through any of the conventional senses. Many people see it as residing in the realm of "imagination," but it would be more appropriate to consider such experiences as housed in a higher "sixth" sense. The good thing is that with enough

exposure, you can be trained to see the little going-ons captured by this sense that you may normally be taking for granted. The specific training we have in this section is fun and relaxing, and can even be used as a form of meditation.

Picture the mind's eye as a huge camera that you can take "pictures" with for later viewing. As of now, you would most probably be seeing everything in your "viewfinder," your physical sense of sight. Try sitting in one place, for example, and memorizing everything as far as you can see. Then, at a later time, try recalling these visuals. Try to immerse yourself in the image and see things as they would appear in real life.

Once you are able to picture the scene as if you were *really* there, then you are on track. You can use the after-image of the visual to help you, touching it up with your mind's eye as it begins to fade. This exercise attempts to merge your "imagination" (the one connected to the sixth sense) with your physical vision. In doing so, you are making a great leap in preparing yourself for visual clairvoyance.

4. **Rev up.** Another analogy is that the mind is like a car that has not seen any mileage for a very long time (if you have read any book about the pineal gland as the third eye, you will see that there's a *very* striking similarity). Many consider that we were all psychics once, but somehow lost the hang of it -- the faculty is there, just not the ability to use it. In this case, it will take more than fixing the senses up with reading and info gathering -- it must be driven to practice, until it can get accustomed to actually running again.

Chapter 3:
The Colors of the Aura

Contrary to what some may say, the colors of a person's aura are not subjective. Because aural perception attunes the observer to the specific state of mind, spirit, or emotion of the person being read, the aural observer will see a chromatic representation that will not vary. This works in the same reason a certain wavelength is colored red to everyone and not just for some -- a certain aural emanation is colored as such for everyone, and not just for a few clairvoyants. This removes that subjective experience that may be evident in other esoteric crafts.

Listed below are the different aural colors and the meanings attached to them. Experienced aural readers may be able to read much more than simply what the colors say -- they may be able to weave a full story depending on the way the colors are displayed, which colors comes from where and their order, as well as how intense the colors are.

- **Red Aura**

    The red aura is connected to the physical body, particularly the circulation, and the heart. Red also pertains to a healthy self-esteem.

    People who display red auras are known to be enthusiastic and brimming with energy. They are always seeking adventure, be it in travel, food, or sex. They're the type of people who are likely to try anything once. That said, this carefree attitude might often get them into trouble. Individuals with red aura have short tempers. They are easily angered and can be unforgiving. On the other hand, they are also generous when it comes to their time and efforts. They are always willing to help their friends.

Red aura individuals are known to be physically and mentally strong. They seldom get sick. For this reason, they tend to excel in sports. A person with a prominent red aura has the tendency to get bored easily. They hop from one idea to another, from one project to another, and from one lover to another. Because of this, they often have trouble in completing tasks. This feature also causes problems in their personal relationships. However, when they do decide to stick to a particular endeavor, they can become extraordinarily successful.

Persons with red auras are direct and bold. They are not afraid to voice out their opinions. They seldom conceal their motives. When dealing with a red aura person, more often than not, what you see is what you get. Red aura individuals have this need to be the best in everything. They are highly competitive and this trait enables them to succeed in life. However, they are not ideal team players and they may have problems in taking orders from authority figures. A person with a red aura would rather be the boss. If not, he'll end up running his own one-man show.

Deep red hues suggest that the person possesses a strong will and has powerful survival instincts. Such people tend to be realistic in their perception of the world.

A clear red aura shows a person who is passionate, powerful, and sensual.

Meanwhile, an orange-red aura indicates self-confidence.

If a person is surrounded by a bright pink aura, then they are artistic, affectionate, sensitive, and compassionate. However, if the person's aura is a dark pink hue, then they may be dishonest or immature.

- **Orange Aura**

   The orange aura is linked to the reproductive organs. It also indicates one's emotions. Orange is the color of vitality.

   People with orange auras are charming and sociable. They like being around others and are often people pleasers. Normally, persons with this aural color possess a good heart. They are in tune to the feelings of others and know how to make others feel comfortable in their company.

   That said, orange aura people possess quick tempers, but unlike red aura people, it's easy for them to forgive and to forget. They are not the type of individuals who carry grudges.

   People with orange auras exude confidence especially regarding the impression that they make on other people. This can be very advantageous for them. Orange aura people have the potential to succeed in life, but because of their impatience, they are used to rushing things, from projects to relationships. They tend to act now and think about the consequences later.

   An orange-yellow aura shows an intelligent, detail-oriented person. Conversely, a brown orange aura reveals a person who is lazy and lacks ambition. Although, this may simply indicate repressed feelings.

- **Pink Aura**

People with predominately pink auras are known to be nature lovers. They possess a giving nature. They enjoy always having their friends and family around them. Pink aura people are health conscious and pay a great deal of attention to diet and exercise.

If you possess a pink aura, then this means that you are a romantic. Pink aura persons are known to be faithful lovers. They are also natural healers since they are sensitive of other people's needs.

If a person has a pink aura, then it's possible for them to possess powerful psychic abilities. They are imaginative and inventive. They may have a future as a novelist, a poet, or a songwriter.

People with pink auras are idealists who abhor the idea of poverty and injustice. They make it their goal to make the world a better place. Pink aura individuals possess strong willpower and they uphold their morals to the end. With that said, they also have high expectations from others. They make honest employees and fair employers.

- **Yellow Aura**

The body organ that the yellow aura is connected to is your spleen. But more than that, the yellow aura is associated with life energy. This color signifies intelligence, inspiration, and optimism.

People who possess yellow auras are believed to be intelligent and analytical. They are best suited to careers related to academics. Most scientists and inventors possess this aural color. Yellow aura individuals tend to be workaholics, causing their personal relationships to suffer.

Persons with yellow auras are often loners who are perfectly fine in their own company. They are also vulnerable to psychological pressure and are prone to suffering from depression.

If your aura is yellow, then you possess excellent communication skills, whether it's in a one-on-one discussion or making a public speech. You have the power to inspire people with your words. You are also gifted with great observation skills. You have the ability to read others' body language.

When it comes to choosing friends, a yellow aura person would rather have a handful of real ones and such friends would have to possess the same level of intellect as his.

In decision-making, persons with yellow auras usually allow their brain to lead rather than their heart. Being nonconformists, they are open to new ideas and are welcome to testing new theories. You'll notice that a yellow aura person's interests tend to be somewhat eclectic and eccentric. They have a fondness for the avant-garde.

A yellow aura person's negative feature is that they may end up being too critical of themselves and of others.

A pale yellow aura reveals someone who is psychic and possesses a high level of spiritual awareness.

However, when you see a bright yellow aura, this may indicate fear. The person may be afraid of losing control. It is also indicative of a power struggle.

A clear metallic gold aura shows an activated spirituality. But a murky yellow gold aura indicates fatigue and mental overload.

- **Green Aura**

Body organs associated with the green aura are the heart and the lungs. Green signifies growth and balance.

If your aura is green, then this means that you are hardworking and brimming with creative power. It's possible too that you're a perfectionist.

Among the positive traits of a green aura person is their determination and down-to-earth nature. They tend to be realistic and practical. A green aura person's creativity is evident in everyday hands-on matters like cooking, gardening, and beautifying the home. They have an eye for beauty and detail and pay attention to their looks as well as their surroundings. They are also a fan of the great outdoors.

Green aura people easily gain the respect and admiration of others. They excel in business and have the potential to generate a great deal of wealth in their lifetime. They like having stability and balance in their lives. They are meticulous planners and are unlikely to make mistakes due to reckless decisions.

When it comes to their friends, the green aura person is loyal and generous. They are also capable of giving sound advice.

An emerald green aura reveals a person who has the potential to heal.

If you see a yellow-green aura, this indicates sincerity as well as creativity.

A forest green aura that appears to be cloudy indicates a person who is jealous, insecure, and sensitive to criticism. They like playing the role of the victim and often blame others for their problems. They are unable to assume personal responsibility.

- **Purple Aura**

    If you happen to observe that your subject's aura is purple, then this indicates possible psychic abilities. Such individuals are sensitive and more attuned to other people's moods. A purple aura also suggests mystery in a person.

    Purple aura people tend to be philosophical. They are inquisitive and intuitive. They enjoy gathering new knowledge. Because of this, they can provide you with interesting company. They tend to keep a small circle of friends, but whatever friends they have, are sure to be loved and respected. When it comes to romance, purple aura individuals may not be the luckiest. But once they've found the person for them, they make loyal lovers for life.

    If a person has a purple aura, they have a strong connection with nature and with animals. It's easy for a purple aura person to sense an animal's aura. Such people often take strays as pets.

- **Violet Aura**

    The violet aural color is connected to your crown chakra. It is associated with your pineal gland and the nervous system. Someone with a violet aura is a true visionary. They have the potential to be skillful in magic and the arts. Violet also shows psychic power. If the aural color is more like lavender, this signifies daydreaming.

- **Blue Aura**

    The blue aura is connected to your thyroid.

    It's rare to see a person with a predominantly blue aura. Such people who radiate this aura have strong personalities. They are charismatic master communicators. They excel in writing and in politics.

    A person with a blue aura possesses high intelligence and intuition. Their mental and emotional faculties are well balanced, enabling them to make good decisions. They have the power to motivate others. They make great mediators in tense situations.

    Blue aura people value straightforwardness, clarity, and truthfulness in their dealings with others. Like yellow aura people, they have a tendency to work too hard and end up sacrificing their relationships.

    A light blue aura shows a peace-loving quality in a person.

A royal blue aura denotes clairvoyance. It also indicates that a person is open to fresh opportunities.

A cloudy blue aural color, on the other hand, reveals fear of expressing one's thoughts and emotions. Similarly, the person may be anxious about the future.

- **Indigo Aura**

   An indigo aura is associated with your third eye and your pituitary gland. This aural color signifies deep feelings.

- **Turquoise Aura**

   A turquoise aura is connected with the immune system. This type of aural color is often seen around healers and therapists as this suggests sensitivity and compassion.

- **Gold Aura**

   A person with a gold aura is artistic and places high value on physical beauty. They like to be surrounded by fine and lovely things as evidenced by their home. They also have a tendency to be extravagant. They are people pleasers and great gift givers, even at times when finances are a little tight. They're not afraid of the limelight, in fact, they thrive in it. They love to be loved by others. Most people find gold aura individuals attractive. Persons with gold auras are also very generous of their time, their energy, and their affection.

   Gold aura persons are great listeners and others find their company exciting. However, people with gold auras loathe criticism and they are fearful of their flaws being exposed. They are very proud and would hate to ask for anybody's help no matter how badly they are in need of it.

- **Silver Aura**

    The silver aura denotes physical wealth as well as spiritual abundance. People who possess this aura are believed to be born gifted. Success comes easily to such individuals. A person with a silver aura is psychic and intuitive. At the same time, they are practical and versatile. They have the ability to relate well with others. For this reason, they may choose the path of a teacher, a mentor, or a counselor.

    Another positive trait of a person with a silver aura is their ability to make the most out of whatever life throws their way. They possess high intellect and though they are quick to make decisions and to take action, they are almost always right.

    People with a silver aural color may attract a great deal of admirers but they choose their company carefully. They are discerning when it comes to choosing lovers as well.

    A person with a bright metallic silver aura possesses a nurturing personality.

    However, if the person's aura looks more like a cloudy gray, this is indicative of accumulated fear. This is also an indicator of physical illness.

    If the subject's aura appears as a dirty gray overlay, this denotes energy blockage. This also suggests suspicion.

- **White Aura**

    A white aural color indicates protection. A person with this aura is believed to be healthy. They are also believed to possess angelic qualities. Flashes of white light are said to be indicators that angels are close by. Conversely, if the person's aura appears to be dirty white or grayish, this is a sign of disease.

- **Black Aura**

    A black aura signifies transforming energy. It also denotes the drawing or the seizing of energy.

    A black aura reveals pent-up hatred or grief and negative thoughts. Nothing good may be said of this aural color. People who are surrounded by a black aura are known to be miserly and unforgiving. The color may also indicate that the person is suffering from a serious sickness or depression. They may also have experienced great problems in their past life.

- **Earth Tone Aura**

    Such aural colors are often seen around people who enjoy working outdoors.

- **Brown Aura**

    If you see this aural color surrounding a person, it may mean that they are confused or not confident about the current situation.

    A dark brown aura also reveals a selfish nature. People with brown auras like finding fault in others. They tend to be close-minded. They are also deceptive individuals.

If the aura appears as a dirty brown overlay, this shows that the person is insecure or that they are holding on to negative energies.

- **Rainbow Tones**

There are also times when a reader can see rainbow-like stripes emanating from a person. Instead of being part of the egg-shaped aura layer, this is mostly seen as beams of multi-colored light. This indicates a potentially powerful healer.

- **Pastel Tones.**

Yes, even pastel tones have meaning! In aura reading, pastel colors mean those soft blends of color and pure light. This is usually seen on sensitive people, and those who need to have peace and serenity in order to function well.

Chapter 4:
How to Feel the Aura

For many of us, seeing the aura as a visual representation might be a tall order. It is known that no matter how hard some may practice, they do not get farther than being able to identify a few basic aural colors -- much like how not everyone can progress to advanced mathematics in school.

For such people, there is an alternative, which is aura "sensing". In fact, it is possible that many of us have unconsciously done it without knowing -- aura sensing has been demonstrated in children as young as four to six years old! Don't you ever wonder why certain children draw people with only a specific color? This is also known as the "vibes" or vibrations that emanate from a person.

First, a disclaimer: though aura sensing is a possible alternative to visually seeing the aura, we would much rather have it as an added skill, a way of counter-checking the validity of the aura colors apparent to your vision.

The most common way to start feeling auras is to feel your *own* aura first. Once you have done so, it is much easier to do the same with others!

The following exercise is a very basic way to help you feel your own aura. Notice that the steps are extremely similar to the steps used in meditation, except that you will not be focusing on your thoughts (or the lack of them). Instead, you will be focusing on your feelings.

1. **Relax.** It helps that you are as relaxed as you can be. It is okay to do the exercise while lying down just before

you go to sleep. Close your eyes and transfer all your consciousness to how and what you feel at the moment.

2. **Do the hand pose.** Rest your arms on something that can take their weight, then bring your hands together just above your belly. This is easiest if your are lying down on your back (just make sure not to fall asleep before you finish the exercise!). The fingertips of each hand should be lightly touching, with the whole hand completely relaxed. The fingers are supposed to naturally bend, resting on each other. After this, your palms should be far enough that you can hold a small ball between them. This will be the start.

3. **Push and pull.** Slowly, pull your hands apart around a few centimeters. Then, push them back together, but do not let the fingertips touch. When they do, the sensation of the aura will be lost. After a few tries, you should be feeling a kind of resistance between your hands as they move towards each other. This is the result of the aura streaming from each of the hands. At the start, it feels like an invisible balloon in between your hands -- the balloon is squeezed every time you bring your hands together.

4. **Concentrate.** Focus all your attention on this balloon, and you will feel the resistance grow more familiar. This is your aura. Once you are used to it (after a few sessions), you may now pull you hands back farther and then back together to feel a bigger portion of your "balloon". Over time, you will learn to consciously attune yourself to the sensation, feeling the aura not only in your hands but in different parts of your body!

This entire process is not a shortcut -- it can take time, each person taking as long as their potential allows them. Of course, it is best to have some sort of background in basic areas of psychism; but when performed regularly, the exercise will help you become aware of the aura surrounding you. Now, it's time to recognize the same in others!

Remember that there are certain factors that can lead an aura field to expand or shrink. These factors include spiritual, emotional, and physical health. Because of these factors, the aura is never permanent, and you might not always be in the right "zone" to properly read aura by sensing. The previous exercise should attune you into recognizing whether you are in contact with another person's aura, so you can start reading it.

The best way to begin when checking other people's auras is to take note of what you feel when you come into their aura zone. This is akin to clairsentience. Record what you feel with all five of your senses -- it will help if you literally record these observations in a logbook or journal. Take note as well of your reactions -- do you feel happy in this person's company? Or maybe you are anxious? Try to discount any other biases you might have against the person and note what colors you would most likely attach to him or her, and in what mixture/layers/intensity.

Over time, as you practice, your senses will grow keener and you'll gradually get closer and closer to the actual aural colors of that person.

Chapter 5:
The Different Layers of The Aura

The physical body is surrounded by seven subtle bodies, also referred to as layers of the aura. These comprise the auric body system. However, as you continue to view inward, you'll find that much unlike most people's idea of layers, each previous aura layer remains to be present within the ensuing aura layer. Thus, as you delve deeper, expect the layers to grow denser and denser. The first and the innermost layer, which is the etheric, contain all of the seven subtle bodies and as such, it is naturally the densest of all the layers.

The seven subtle bodies comprise of:

- three physical plane bodies (lower bodies)

- three spiritual plane bodies (higher bodies)

- and one astral body

The latter serves as a link between the lower and the higher bodies.

In order to be effectively utilized by the lower bodies, the energies from the higher planes must first go through one's heart chakra. It is important to know that all seven layers of the aura possess their own seven chakras. Chakras can be seen as vortexes of energy vertically aligned in the body. Chakras allow us to tap into the free-floating energy in the universe, enabling us to sustain ourselves. In each auric layer, each of the chakras is embedded within the other auric chakras. The chakras of the outer aural layers vibrate at a higher frequency. As you extend inwards, the vibrational frequency becomes lower. Thus, the etheric body is expected to vibrate at the lowest rate.

Viewing all aura layers entails a great deal of practice. There are aura readers who are unable to view the whole set of bodies at one time. If your goal is to eventually heal someone or yourself, then it is imperative that you be able to identify one layer from the other.

The Etheric Body

This is known as the first layer of the aura. This field vibrates closely to the physical body. It is an indicator of your physical health. The first layer extends 1 and ¼ inch to 2 inches outward with a pulsation of fifteen to twenty cycles per minute. It can be perceived as either a bluish light which indicates being emotional, or a grayish light which suggests being very active. When reading this layer, you may feel either one of two things: pain or pleasure. It is connected to the root chakra.

The Emotional Body

Like the etheric, the emotional body is naturally fluid and does not follow the body. This field extends 1- 3 inches from the physical body. This second layer is linked to your feelings and as such, it does not possess a single color. Instead, it can be perceived as rainbow-colored and constantly changing. The dominant color will depend on the emotions that a person is currently experiencing. Feelings of love, happiness, anger, or excitement will reveal bright colors whereas negative emotions and emotional blocks result in more opaque hues. Any problems in this field will inevitably impact both the etheric body and the mental body. This layer is linked with your sacral chakra.

The Mental Body

The third layer extends 3 – 8 inches from the physical body. It contains a person's thoughts as well as their mental processes. It is usually perceived as a yellow light radiating from around one's head and shoulders and extending downward toward the body. If the subject is deep in concentration, the light tends to grow brighter. With that being said, any emotions arising from the emotional body might also alter the color of the mental body.

The Astral Layer

This fourth layer, extending to around six inches from the physical body, is the bridge to the spiritual plane. This is also your gateway to the Astral Plane. Working within and above this field will enable you to perceive energies that are not within the vibrational frequency of the physical realm. The Astral Plane is where spirits and angels transition to other planes. Compared to the physical plane, it vibrates on a higher frequency.

The colors associated with the fourth layer can be described as beautiful and rainbow-like. Vibrant rainbow colors are indicative of good spiritual health. In an affectionate person, a pinkish hue may often be present, accompanying the other rainbow colors. This plane has strong links to your heart chakra as well as to the emotional body. As such, people in love have pink light radiating from their heart chakras.

The Etheric Template Body

This fifth layer contains a blueprint, which holds all the forms of the physical realm. It extends about one-half to two feet outward. In case the lower etheric body becomes disfigured, this field becomes essential to healing. It is perceived as a dark blue tint. That said, due to the fact that it creates negative space, the colors may differ. This is linked to the throat charka, which is associated with communication and creativity.

The Celestial Body

The sixth layer is a spiritual-emotional plane. This is where you experience powerful emotions such as bliss and spiritual rapture. This is the seat of divine love and oneness with the universe experienced during advanced meditation. In raising your level of consciousness to this sixth field, you are enabling a connection to occur between the heart and the celestial chakras. Whereas the heart chakra allows you to love, the celestial chakra transcends that emotion into unconditional love. The sixth layer is seen in opalescent pastel hues. This layer is connected to the brow chakra, which is associated with dreams and the workings of the subconscious mind.

The Causal Body or the Ketheric Template

The seventh field is known as the spiritual-mental plane. Extending from three to three-and-a-half-feet from the physical body, the Causal Body holds all of the other bodies within it. This body surrounds the other fields and binds them together, much like a skin for all the other auras. It pulsates and vibrates at the highest frequency. It can be seen as a strong grid-like structure with threads of golden hues. Sometimes, it appears as silver-gold filaments. It is linked to the crown chakra and is associated with the highest level of spiritual evolution. At this level, we are one with the divine. It also reveals all of the experiences and events that have been encountered by one's soul.

Chapter 6:
Strategies for Seeing Auras

Basic Technique for Seeing Auras

The first thing that you need to know is that auras are not to be looked at. Instead, they are to be gazed upon.

- To begin your training, you'll need soft and good light such as a 100 watt bulb coming from behind and above you. Avoid harsh lighting or anything reflecting into your eyes. Light pouring in from a window, for instance, may serve as a distraction and prevent you from seeing an aura clearly.

- Prior to training, relax and ground yourself. Don't try too hard and avoid straining your eyes and your brain as this will have a counter effect.

- Select a subject. Human auras are very complex so it would be wise to begin your training with an inanimate object. Not everyone knows this but colors have their own auras. You may begin with sensing the aura of a piece of paper in the primary color (either *bright* red or *bright* blue because they are easiest to use). Find a solid object and cover it with blue or red paper, a brick, for instance, or a book. Then place it upright on a table. The distance should be at least two meters away from you. Alternatively, you may choose to simply hang a piece of colored paper on the wall. That said, a neutral background such as a white wall or a wall covered in a white sheet is recommended for this.

- The next step is to close your eyes and take a few deep and relaxing breaths. Then, open your eyes and look at the subject. Do not allow your eyes to specifically focus on anything. *Gaze* a little to the side of the subject and behind it, almost as though you are directing your attention to the backdrop. This is done to enable your eyes to relax. At the same time, this allows you to view the subject through your peripheral vision. Understand that what peripheral vision means here is not seeing out of the corner of your eye, rather, this means looking past an object a couple of inches to the side.

- Now hold that gaze and allow your eyes to relax. This should be a relaxed and steady concentration (as though you are daydreaming) as opposed to an intense focus. What if you have to blink? Will an aura disappear when you blink? Yes. But often, it instantly reappears after a couple of seconds. To prevent your eyes from straining, watering or burning, blink if you need to but don't allow this to change your focus.

- Next, direct all of your bodily awareness to your brow or the zone between your eyes. With your fingernail, mildly scratch the skin between your eyes. Think of a time when you felt very tired and had to battle with your eyelids so that you may keep your eyes open. Remember the sensation that it created, as though you were trying to lift a heavy veil behind your eyes. In such instances, since the tired eye muscles fail to cooperate, the action becomes entirely mental instead of physical. All of your bodily awareness is concentrated on your brow area and so you are able to mentally manipulate that area. Each time you perform this kind of mental action, your brow area, the seat of your third eye, is stimulated. Remember that in the same way as the eyes are the physical organ for optic vision, the brow center is the non-physical organ for non-physical vision. This is known as the third eye.

- Now, using your mind and without engaging the muscles, practice mentally lifting your eyelids several times. Meanwhile, maintain your relaxed gaze beyond and to the side of the object. Do not lose your focus but at the same time, refrain from looking directly at the subject.

- Eventually, the aura will appear. If you used blue paper, you will see a bright yellow aura. If you used red paper, you will see a bright green aura. The color will emerge from the pale etheric band surrounding the subject. At this point, it is important to remain relaxed and to avoid looking at the subject directly. Otherwise, the aura will vanish.

- When you're done with this exercise, it's time to level up. Use different primary colors (red, blue, and yellow) as your subjects. First, observe the subjects one at a time and then note the colors that appear. Then, observe the subjects two at a time and compare the color of their auras. Lastly, observe all the subjects together and see how their auras differ.

- When you're able to view the auras of inanimate objects, it's time to move on to viewing the auras of animate objects. It's easiest to start with potted plants or fresh flowers. You will observe an orange color. This comes from the green parts of the plant (leaves and stems). Any other colors that you will see will be coming from the other parts of the plant. The hues that you will notice around the flowers and petals will depend entirely upon their color. You'll find that living auras are a little more difficult to see since they are more subtle. When attempting to view the aura of living things, look for the band of etheric energy. The next and the bigger layer after this is the aura.

- When you're able to see a living aura, the next step would be to practice viewing the aura of a tree. For this exercise, choose a tree that is highlighted against the sky. The top of the tree should be visible in your field of vision. Do this with the sun situated behind you. Its light should not be in your eyes. You'll find that the light radiating around a tree is more intense compared to the light that you'll see in potted plants. The leaves, the bark, and even the sky all contribute to the auric color that you will see surrounding the tree. As does the tree's age, size, and strength. If you perform this exercise on a fair day, the tree's aura may be blue. On a cloudy day, expect the color to be grayish. If you see a fountain-like light spraying up out of the top of the tree, you are seeing its spirit.

With sufficient practice, you can move on to viewing the auras of animals and of human beings as well as your own.

Seeing the Aura of Others

Once you're certain that you're ready to see other people's auras, then it would be best for you to begin practicing with a partner. Follow the same instructions in viewing the aura of inanimate objects.

- Have your partner stand about eighteen inches from a plain wall.

- Look directly above the top of and beyond your subject's head. Keep your gaze on the wall, about two inches away from the subject's body.

- Soon, you will begin to see an energy outline surrounding your subject. You will notice that a certain part of the background appears to be lighter than the rest. Try to determine the specific color.

- After you are able to view this, ask the subject to sway from side to side. As they do this, the energy field should follow their movements. On the other hand, an after-image will not follow the subject's movement. Instead, what will cause it to move is the movement of your own eyes. You will notice that an after-image is of the opposite color of the person's aura.

Other things to remember:

- The colors around your subject such as clothing and other objects in the room can influence an aura. It is therefore important that you trust your instincts in identifying which parts of your vision are associated with the surroundings rather than with the energy springing out of your subject.

- Do not mistake the etheric body (seen as a thin white strip) for an aura. With a little more practice, you will finally be able to perceive the actual aura.

- Your own energy may interfere with your ability to see an aura. Prior to attempting aura viewing, ensure that you are clear, positive, and prepared.

Chapter 7:
Auras of Different Things and Animals

As learned from the previous chapter, animals and even inanimate objects do possess auras. Auras are a representation of an animal's emotions. But more than that, they also represent the creature's life force. You'll notice that auras in conscious objects have a tendency to change constantly. It is inevitable for the auras of living things to change overtime. On the other hand, auras of non-living objects tend to be fixed. However, you have the potential to change them with your conscious intent. Furthermore, each time something or someone comes in contact with another being (living or non-living), a psychic signature is left behind. For this reason, some inanimate objects may show many different auras. In reality, these are the auras of living things that have come in contact with them at one point or another.

Sensing your Pet's Aura

Ever wonder why pet whisperers are so good at their job? A great number of animal communicators have the ability to view and interpret the auras of animals so that they are able to determine what they want and to detect any illnesses that they are suffering from. You too can possess the ability to sense your pet's aura so that you can be in tune with what they're feeling. Compared to the auras of human beings, animal auras are not as complex. This is because their feelings and thoughts are simpler in comparison to ours. For this reason, you may see only one or two colors close to your pet's body. When your pet is happy, you may see a shiny, splashy-looking aura. On the other hand, if they're upset, you will see a cloudy color accompanied by black, gray, or dark brown hues. The presence of black holes indicates that the animal is unwell.

- To view your pet's aura, you need to wait until they are relaxed or feeling sleepy. With that said, *you* need to relax and focus as well.

- Without touching your pet/the animal, sit or stand comfortably near it. Place your hands 12 inches away from your pet's head. Focus your eyes a little above your pet.

- Then observe the first sensation that comes to you. Keeping your distance, allow your hands to float and to roam slowly over your pet's body. Allow your intuition to tell you where to linger. You will be able to feel where the energy activity is the strongest.

- It may help to breathe in your pet's scent. Now visualize: How would your pet perceive the world? What would it be like to be in your pet's shoes?

- Lastly, in your mind's eye, create a protective coat made out of light. Wrap your pet and your pet's aura in this colored cloak of protection. Then, withdraw yourself.

- If you have access to animals, which are not usually considered as pets, you may practice aura reading on them as well. Maintain a safe distance and keep in mind that the color of the animal's coat may greatly affect the aural color.

Chapter 8:
How to Change and Improve Your Aura

There are many methods that you can employ to strengthen your aura and to change a negative aura to a positive aura.

- **Have a yogic cleansing bath.** Doing so will help get rid of the negativities from your aura, not to mention wash away the toxins from your physical body.

    Add one pound of baking soda and one cup of sea salt into your bath water. Soak for at least twenty minutes every day for one week.

    Note: Get out of the bath once you experience symptoms of dizziness.

- **Inhale white sage smoke.** This is performed to cleanse your aura. After lighting the sage smudge stick, use your hands to direct the smoke towards your face and all over your body.

- **Bask under the sun**. This is done to fuel your aura, enabling it to expand. Spend time outdoors and be one with nature. Sunlight will replenish your energy and fill you with optimism.

- **Use crystals.** Tears in the auric field may occur during periods of extreme stress. Sometimes, they are caused by childbirth or major surgery. The crystal Labradorite is known to be effective in preventing leakage and patching up tears in the auric field. Healers use this stone for protection so if you are a healthcare worker, a childcare worker, or a teacher, invest in this crystal.

Hold it for twenty minutes a day. Its protective effect can last for up to twelve hours. An Amethyst and Citrine bracelet worn for half a year is also used for healing the holes in the auric field.

Black Tourmaline is another protective crystal that's worth mentioning. It can deflect radiation and transmute negative energy from your aura. If you are plagued with negative thoughts, keep this crystal in your purse or pocket and carry it with you wherever you go. A Kunzite is also useful in banishing negative thoughts. If you wish to shield yourself from other people's stresses, keep a Smoky Quartz on your office desk or beside the phone. If you want to strengthen your aura, try using Amber.

- **Use essential oils.** Apply a few drops of Vetiver on your belly button. This will protect you from absorbing other people's negativity. This essential oil calms and grounds you, especially after sitting for several hours in front of the computer screen. Furthermore, this oil influences your chakras so that they become perfectly aligned.

- **Chant.** Sound is a healing tool used by old cultures to cleanse one's energies. Chanting "Om" while meditating moves the stagnant negative energy from the aura.

- **Take flower essences.** Angelsword is known to repair impaired auric fields. You may take it per orem or you may instill several drops of the essence into your solar plexus before bedtime.

- **Avoid overexposure to electrical gadgets.** This is because they emit radiation, and man-made frequencies can create disturbances in the auric field. Your bedroom should be free from electrical gadgets. Do not sleep with your mobile phone! If your job requires you to spend several hours a day in front of a computer, invest in a Lepidolite crystal because it can create a protective field that can shield you from the harmful effects of electrical devices.

Chapter 9:
How to See Your Own Aura

Seeing Your Own Aura

- Prior to attempting to visualize your own aura, prepare yourself through meditation. It is important that your mind and body be relaxed.

- Begin by standing or sitting in front of a mirror. Your background should be plain, preferably white. Make sure that you perform this under soft and indirect lighting.

- Then, close your eyes and take several deep breaths. Feel the air as it moves in and out of your body.

- Next, gradually open your eyes. Gaze at your reflection in the mirror. Your gaze should be somewhat out of focus.

- Allow your eyes to rest at the area around your body. Refrain from looking at yourself directly. Basically, you are applying the same rules in viewing the auras of inanimate objects.

- Eventually, you will see a glowing light surrounding your body. Try to identify the color. If the light disappears, just relax and allow your eyes to readjust.

- The next step would be to view the aura surrounding your hands. To do this, assume a standing position with your back to the source of light. You should be standing directly in front of a darker room. Slowly, bring your fingertips together.

- Afterwards, gradually pull your hands apart. Your gaze should be resting on the space between your fingertips. There you will see flashes of white energy.

Conclusion

Thank you again for downloading this book!

I hope this book was able to help you learn more about auras and what they mean!

The next step is to put this information to use, and begin seeing and interpreting auras!

Also don't forget to download my **FREE** report on the 7 Keys for Successful Meditation by following the link - http://bit.ly/1F91lfl

Finally, if you enjoyed this book, please take the time to share your thoughts and post a review on Amazon. It'd be greatly appreciated!

Thank you and good luck!

www.ingramcontent.com/pod-product-compliance
Lightning Source LLC
LaVergne TN
LVHW021742060526
838200LV00052B/3416